DISCOVER 🐾 DOGS WITH
THE AMERICAN CANINE ASSOCIATION

I LIKE
BOXERS!

Linda Bozzo

It is the mission of the American Canine Association (ACA) to provide registered dog owners with the educational support needed for raising, training, showing, and breeding the healthiest pets expected by responsible pet owners throughout the world. Through our activities and services, we encourage and support the dog world in order to promote best-known husbandry standards as well as to ensure that the voice and needs of our customers are quickly and properly addressed.

Our continued support, commitment, and direction are guided by our customers, including veterinary, legal, and legislative advisors. ACA aims to provide the most efficient, cooperative, and courteous service to our customers and strives to set the standard for education and problem solving for all who depend on our services.

For more information, please visit www.acacanines.com, e-mail customerservice@acadogs.com, phone 1-800-651-8332, or write to the American Canine Association at PO Box 121107, Clermont, FL 34712.

Published in 2018 by Enslow Publishing, LLC.
101 W. 23rd Street, Suite 240, New York, NY 10011

Library of Congress Cataloging-in-Publication Data

Names: Bozzo, Linda, author.
Title: I like boxers! / Linda Bozzo.
Description: New York : Enslow Publishing, 2018. | Series: Discover dogs with the American Canine Association | Includes bibliographical references and index. | Audience: Grades K to 3.
Identifiers: LCCN 2017001304 | ISBN 9780766086388 (library-bound) | ISBN 9780766088788 (pbk.) | ISBN 9780766088726 (6-pack)
Subjects: LCSH: Boxer (Dog breed)—Juvenile literature.
Classification: LCC SF429.B75 B69 2017 | DDC 636.73—dc23
LC record available at https://lccn.loc.gov/2017001304

Printed in the United States of America

To Our Readers: We have done our best to make sure all websites in this book were active and appropriate when we went to press. However, the author and the publisher have no control over and assume no liability for the material available on those websites or on any websites they may link to. Any comments or suggestions can be sent by email to customerservice@enslow.com.

Photo Credits: Cover, p. 1 Susan Schmitz/Shutterstock.com; p. 3 (left), 17 Lyubov Timofeyeva/Shutterstock.com; p. 3 (right) Noska Photo/Shutterstock.com; p. 5 lewkmiller/iStock/Thinkstock; p. 6 Jana Behr/Shutterstock.com; p. 9 hjalmeida/iStock/Thinkstock; p. 10 Anna Hoychuk/Shutterstock.com; p. 13 (left) vdovin_vn/Shutterstock.com; p. 13 (collar) graphicphoto/iStock/Thinkstock, (bed) Luisa Leal Photography/Shutterstock.com, (brush) gvictoria/Shutterstock.com, (food and water bowls) exopixel/Shutterstock.com, (leash, toys) © iStockphoto.com/Liliboas; p. 14 Mikhail Ter-avanesov/Hemera/Thinkstock; p. 18 Jetta Productions/DigitalVision/Getty Images; p. 19 © iStockphoto.com/tzahiV; p. 21 Michael Lofenfeld/Shutterstock.com.

Enslow Publishing
101 W. 23rd Street
Suite 240
New York, NY 10011
USA
enslow.com

CONTENTS

IS A BOXER RIGHT FOR YOU?

Boxers are friendly dogs. They like being with **active** families. Boxers do best in homes with lots of space to play.

Because boxers are strong dogs and like to jump, they need to be watched around small children and the elderly.

A DOG OR A PUPPY?

Firm but kind training for boxers should start when they are very young. If you do not have time to train a puppy, an older boxer may be better in your home.

Your boxer puppy will grow to be medium to large in size.

Even older boxers are likely to be playful.

LOVING YOUR BOXER

Boxers like to have fun and make you laugh. Your boxer will want to spend a lot of time with you. Love your boxer by cuddling with him. Play with him and give him treats.

EXERCISE

Boxers need plenty of walking every day on a **leash.** Full of energy, boxers are always ready to play games, like **fetch.**

Boxers need a large yard with a high fence to play in.

FEEDING YOUR BOXER

Boxers can be fed wet or dry dog food. Ask a **veterinarian** (vet), a doctor for animals, which food is best for your dog and how much to feed her.

Give your boxer fresh, clean water every day.

Remember to keep your dog's food and water dishes clean. Dirty dishes can make a dog sick.

Do not feed your dog people food. It can make her sick.

Your new dog will need:

a collar with a tag

a bed

a brush

food and water dishes

a leash

toys

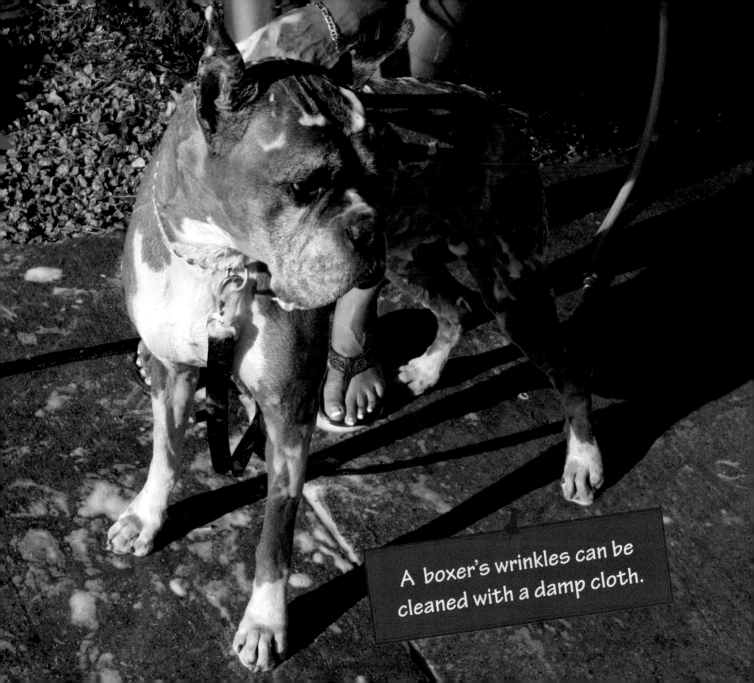

A boxer's wrinkles can be cleaned with a damp cloth.

GROOMING

Boxers do **shed**. This means their hair falls out. These dogs need very little brushing to keep their short coats clean and looking great.

Your dog will need a bath every so often. Use a gentle soap made just for dogs. A boxer's nails need to be clipped. A vet or **groomer** can show you how. Your dog's ears should be cleaned and her teeth should be brushed by an adult.

WHAT YOU SHOULD KNOW

White boxers may be born deaf.

Boxers need to be kept cool in the summer and warm in the winter.

This breed makes a good watchdog.

Boxers have lots of energy.

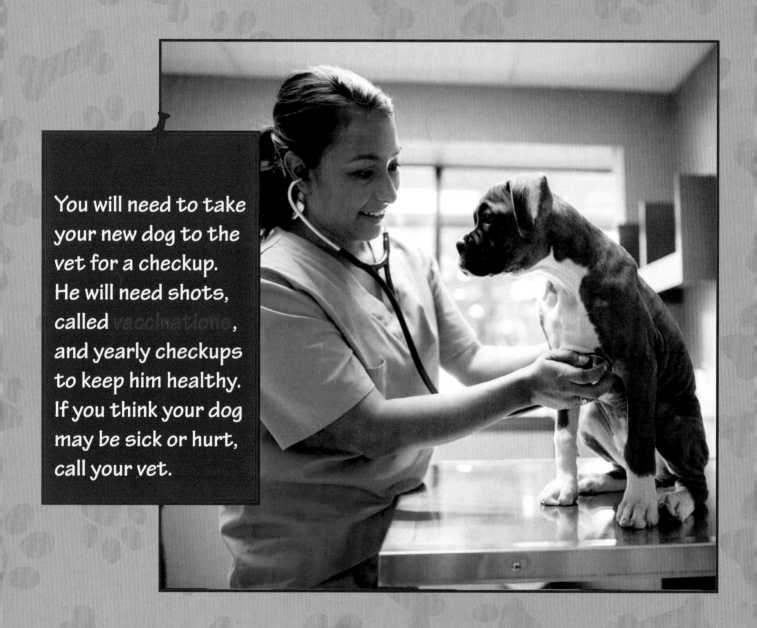

You will need to take your new dog to the vet for a checkup. He will need shots, called vaccinations, and yearly checkups to keep him healthy. If you think your dog may be sick or hurt, call your vet.

A GOOD FRIEND

Like a good friend your boxer will keep you smiling for a long time. Boxers can live up to twelve years.

NOTE TO PARENTS

It is important to consider having your dog spayed or neutered when the dog is young. Spaying and neutering are operations that prevent unwanted puppies and can help improve the overall health of your dog.

It is also a good idea to microchip your dog, in case he or she gets lost. A vet will implant a microchip under the skin containing an identification number that can be scanned at a vet's office or animal shelter. The microchip registry is contacted and the company uses the ID number to look up your information from a database.

Some towns require licenses for dogs, so be sure to check with your town clerk.

For more information, speak with a vet.

There are many dogs, young and old, waiting to be adopted from animal shelters and rescue groups.

active Always doing something.

fetch To go after a toy and bring it back.

groomer A person who bathes and brushes dogs.

leash A chain or strap that attaches to the dog's collar.

shed When dog hair falls out so new hair can grow.

vaccinations Shots that dogs need to stay healthy.

veterinarian (vet) A doctor for animals.

Books

Hansen, Grace. *Boxers* (Dogs). Minneapolis, MN: Abdo Kids, 2016.

Schuh, Mari. *Boxers* (Awesome Dogs). Minnetonka, MN: Bellweather Media, 2016.

Statts, Leo. *Boxers* (Zoom in on Dogs). Minneapolis, MN: Abdo Zoom, 2016.

Websites

American Canine Association Inc., Kids Corner
www.acakids.com
Visit the official website of the American Canine Association.

National Geographic for Kids, Pet Central
kids.nationalgeographic.com / explore / pet-central
Learn more about dogs and other pets at the official site of the National Geographic Society for Kids.

INDEX